Bitesize theology

Bitesize theology

Peter Jeffery

EVANGELICAL PRESS

EVANGELICAL PRESS
Faverdale North Industrial Estate, Darlington, DL3 0PH, England

Evangelical Press USA
P. O. Box 84, Auburn, MA 01501, USA

e-mail: sales@evangelical-press.org

web: www.evangelical-press.org

First published 2000
Second impression February 2001
Third impression June 2002

British Library Cataloguing in Publication Data available

ISBN 0 85234 447 3

Printed and bound in Great Britain by Cox & Wyman Ltd, Reading.

Contents

Introduction

A pastor in the USA once complained that many Christian writers seem unable to put the cookies where the people can reach them. He went on to say that, in his opinion, they forget that they are supposed to be feeding sheep and not giraffe! Many a young believer who has struggled through a book on doctrine would sympathize with that.

I hope that the 'cookies' in this book will be easily accessible to all believers, and that the truths they convey will feed their minds with the riches of God's grace and nourish their hearts with a greater knowledge of the Lord Jesus Christ.

I.
ABC

The writer of the book to the Hebrews was disturbed and disappointed that his readers had not yet grasped the elementary truths of the faith (Hebrews 5:11-14). Spiritual milk was all they were capable of digesting: they could not cope with solid food. I wonder what he would have thought of many Christians at the beginning of the twenty-first century who are almost totally doctrinally illiterate.

Being slow to learn is not a matter of lack of intelligence but of lack of spiritual hunger and desire. Neither is it always a matter of lack of opportunity to receive teaching. From Hebrews 5 it appears that both spiritual milk and meat were available but they were content to stay on the milk. Their immaturity had nothing to do with how long they had been saved but it was a result of unbelief and not using the opportunities God had placed before them. They had been taught the elementary truths of the faith but they had either not understood these (Hebrews 5:11) or they had forgotten them (2 Peter 1:9), so they needed this teaching to be given to them all over again.

Without the basic building blocks, without the ABC, it is impossible to make any progress. If William Shakespeare had not learned and mastered the ABC of the English language he could never have written his masterpieces. Of course Shakespeare had other literary gifts and talents, but without the ABC he could never have written anything. In the same way, the ABC of the faith has to be mastered if Christians are to grow spiritually. We will not mature merely by reading the spiritual experiences of others, important though these are. Doctrine is simply a word to describe what the Bible teaches and no believer should be afraid to grapple with it.

The place of preaching

Christians are often put off doctrine by the sort of preaching they hear.

The heavy, boring and dry teaching that goes half a metre above the heads of its hearers is deadly. It may be biblically orthodox but it simply never reaches the people. It is presented in a manner that never seems to take in mind its hearers. The preacher may be having a fine time but he is not in the pulpit for that. His business ought to be to glorify God, to edify the minds and to warm the hearts of the people before him. Doctrinal preaching, because of the subjects it is dealing with, ought to be thrilling to hear and should excite the hearts and minds of God's people. There is no greater inducement to want to understand the doctrines of the faith, than to hear preaching of these truths that is both warm and passionate.

In contrast to this is the kind of preaching that is full of stories and jokes but has little or no content. It is easy to listen to but it leaves its hearers with no awareness of the glory and majesty of God. It is entertaining but it does not create in the people a deeper love for Christ. It is popular but just as useless as the passionless doctrinal sermon because it fails to address the minds of the people.

What is the ABC?

The ABC of the faith does not mean simple doctrines as opposed to more difficult truths. The writer to the Hebrews considered the elementary truths to be 'the foundation of repentance from acts that lead to death, and of faith in God, instruction about baptisms, the laying on of hands, the resurrection of the dead, and eternal judgement' (Hebrews 6:1-2). We may be tempted to think that these are far from elementary, but that is how the first-century church regarded them.

There are not two sets of doctrines in the Bible, one called milk and the other called meat, one for new believers and the other for more mature saints. There is only one body of truth and all believers, young or old in the faith, need it all. The ABC is doctrine presented in a more basic and easy-to-understand way. Every Christian needs to understand the difference between justification and sanctification, and such biblical doctrines can be taught with understanding to Christian teenagers. Indeed there is no doctrine in the Bible that Christian youngsters do not need to know and love. But there is a difference in teaching doctrine to a young people's fellowship and to a ministers' conference. The difference is not in subject matter but in depth and application. It is not a matter of watering down the doctrine to make it more acceptable but of explaining it in a way that makes it understandable to young believers.

In this book we intend to deal with biblical doctrine in a way that will enlighten those who are immature in the faith and create in them a hunger to know more. In doing this I hope to be brief, simple and accurate. Some of the material I have taken from a couple of my other books. I have tried to put all the doctrinal cookies on the same plate so that they are easily accessible.

It's *worth quoting*

'We are to preach Christ in the fulness of his being and grace. We are to hold nothing back which God has revealed … it should be our goal to tell as much about Jesus Christ as we possibly can. The Holy Spirit will bless such faithful teaching. He will use the doctrines of his word to convict and convert those destined for salvation. God saves through theology' (Edward Donnelly).

Further reading

Sinclair Ferguson, *Handle with Care,* Hodder & Stoughton

2.
Big words

Some Christians think of doctrine as being big words; words they can hardly spell, let alone understand. They think of words like propitiation and justification as being well beyond the understanding of ordinary Christians. It is true that these are big words. The truths they express are gigantic in their importance and massive in their place at the heart of the Christian faith. But it ought not to be beyond the ability of most believers to understand them, especially when we remember that Paul used these words in writing to the church in Rome and most of the Christians there had nothing like the educational advantages we have. The Apostle expected the Romans to understand propitiation and justification and he would have been amazed at our protests that these big words are too much for us.

Most of the New Testament doctrinal words are technical words; that is, they have a special significance and meaning for Christianity. Just about every activity of men and women has its own peculiar vocabulary. A man would not be much of a musician if he did not understand the difference between a crochet and a quaver. And youngsters with their computers all know what a mega-bite and

CD-ROM are. Even sport has its special vocabulary — soccer has its back-four, golf its birdies and pars, cricket its maiden over and tennis its 15-love. The followers of these activities all know the vocabulary because they love what they are doing and constant use of the words make them familiar. Surely it is not unreasonable to expect Christians to know the vocabulary of what they believe. Doctrinal words are the technical words of the Christian faith.

Maybe modern translations of the Bible have made us lazy. Personally I am all for a good modern translation, providing it is accurate. For most Christians it is an advantage to remove the archaisms that have nothing to do with the original texts, but if we try to get rid of the technical words of doctrine in the Bible we may well change the meaning too. For instance, 'propitiation' is used in the Authorised Version of the Bible, in the New King James Version and in the American Standard Version, but the New International Version translates it as 'sacrifice of atonement'. This is alright as far as it goes, but it does not do full justice to what propitiation means. Propitiation also carries with it the meaning that God's wrath upon our sin is turned away or appeased by Christ's sacrifice on the cross. It would be better to retain all the old technical words and for Christians to get to know exactly what they are trying to convey to us. One or two word changes cannot do justice to these big and great words.

Young believers may appreciate a brief definition of the big Bible words and these can be found at the end of the book. But be warned that brief definitions of words like grace, sanctification and election are rarely adequate. The chapters on these words are brief because this book is not intended for mature believers but to introduce doctrine to those Christians who are bewildered by it.

It's *worth quoting*

'To understand spiritual truth, and to be sure of understanding it, is to make a person a spiritual millionaire — but the tragedy today is that so many people in and out of the church are so spiritually impoverished that they could qualify for supplementary benefit if such a thing was available' (John Blanchard).

3.
God

If our thinking about God is not correct then every other doctrine we apply our minds to will also be incorrect. This is the most important doctrine yet people seem to think they are free to make up their minds as to what God is like. So some who call themselves Christians say, 'My god would never send anyone to hell.' Such a statement is only possible if you ignore all that the Bible has to say and just impose your own thoughts on the subject. This attitude is responsible for what is possibly the greatest sin a person can commit — to reduce God to terms that are acceptable to us (Psalm 50:21). This is why in the Old Testament one of the sins that grieved God the most was idolatry. This is to substitute man-made objects and ideas in the place of the one true God (Jeremiah 10:3-5). It is a slander on the character of God and all worship that flows from it is worthless.

What is God like?

The answer to this question is that he is not like anything we have known or experienced. In Isaiah we find God

challenging us on this question: 'To whom will you compare me or count me equal? To whom will you liken me
that we may be compared?' (46:5). The psalmist does the
same thing: 'For who in the skies above can compare with
the Lord? Who is like the Lord among the heavenly beings?' (89:6).

If this is true, how can we know anything about God?
We must go to the place where God has chosen to reveal
himself to us. We must go to the Bible. In the Bible we
discover the attributes of God. An attribute is anything
God has chosen to tell us about himself. We need to know
these things for two reasons. Firstly, if God has been so
gracious to show us something about himself, then we need
to receive all he gives; and secondly, because the study of
God is the highest and greatest subject that can occupy
the mind of a Christian.

God is holy

The truth we are told more than anything else in Scripture
about God is that he is holy (Psalm 99:9; 119:9; Revelation 15:4). This means that he is free from all sin and evil
and there is in him absolute moral perfection. This particular truth touches everything else, so that God's love is
a holy love; his justice is a holy justice; his wrath a holy
wrath. God can do nothing that is not holy.

This is an awesome truth but also a comforting one
because the salvation he provides for us is a holy salvation.
There is no fault or blemish in it; therefore there is no possibility of it failing.

God is sovereign

This means the absolute rule and authority of God over his creation (1 Chronicles 29:11-12). He has the power to carry out his will and purposes. God is no fairy-tale king who can only look on helplessly as his enemies triumph. He is omnipotent (has all power), omniscient (has all knowledge), omnipresent (is in all places). He can do what he likes, when he likes, how he likes and with whom he likes (Job 23:13).

What a comfort and joy to know that this is our God!

The God of providence

He is always at work in the lives of his people so nothing happens to us by chance or luck. God upholds, guides and governs all circumstances (Genesis 41:22). Sometimes it is difficult for us to see this, but Paul tells us that God 'works out everything in conformity with the purpose of his will' (Ephesians 1:11).

It was belief in this great truth about God that brought peace and contentment to Paul in difficult times.

God is good

God is good, he is kind and generous, tender-hearted and full of sympathy (Psalm 145:9,15-16). There is nothing harsh or unreasonable about him, but God's goodness is not weakness or softness. He is not some soft touch that people can take advantage of.

For his people this goodness means that we can rely on God; we can trust him and know that whatever circumstances we will have to face, God will use them for our good and well-being.

God is love

If God was not love there would be no hope for any of us. Divine love is not a sloppy, sentimental thing but a love that acts on behalf of its recipients.

> It is undeserved love (Romans 5:6-8)
> It is unsought love (1 John 4:10)
> It is unimaginable love (1 John 3:1)

There are many, many other truths about God that the Bible reveals to us and we shall see more of them later in this book. But for the moment these are enough to lay the foundation of all that is to follow. Every biblical doctrine originates in the heart and mind of God. Every doctrine is rich in expounding the character of God, and every one of them will deepen our love for God.

It's *worth quoting*

'Nothing will so enlarge the intellect, nothing so magnify the whole soul of man, as a devout, earnest, continued investigation of the great subject of the Deity. Would you lose your sorrow? Would you drown your cares? Then go, plunge yourself in the Godhead's deepest sea; be lost in his immensity; and you shall come forth as from a couch of rest, refreshed and invigorated. I know nothing which can so comfort the soul; so calm the swelling billows of sorrow and grief; so speak peace to the winds of trial, as a devout musing upon the subject of the Godhead' (C. H. Spurgeon).

Think about it

1. Why should people want to worship such useless gods as described in Jeremiah 10?
2. Is idolatry a thing of the past?
3. How would you explain Romans 8:28 to someone in sorrow over the death of a loved one?
4. Why does the Bible emphasize so much the holiness of God?

Further reading

Peter Jeffery, *Great God of Wonders*, Evangelical Press

4.
Jesus

The question of who Jesus is, is crucial to the validity of the Christian faith. It was a question important to Jesus himself, so in Matthew 16 we find him asking his disciples, 'Who do people say the Son of Man is?' The answers are interesting and if spoken of any other person would be highly flattering. Common opinion held that Jesus was either John the Baptist, Elijah or Jeremiah. People were so impressed with him that they thought he must be one of these great servants of God come back from the dead. Flattering though the answers were, they were totally inadequate to describe who Jesus is; the Bible leaves us in no doubt as to the uniqueness and exclusiveness of Jesus.

- 'He is the image of the invisible God, the firstborn over all creation. For by him all things were created' (Colossians 1:15-16).
- 'In Christ all the fulness of the Deity lives in bodily form' (Colossians 2:9).
- 'The Son is the radiance of God's glory and the exact representation of his being' (Hebrews 1:3).

Jesus is special

Nothing like this is said of any other person in Scripture. All other men and women are sinners. We are born with a sinful nature and our actions are all tainted by this nature. If Jesus was only the greatest man who ever lived, he would have had a sinful nature and as such he would *need* a saviour and could never have *been* Saviour.

Jesus is special. His birth was special and different from all other births. His mother Mary was a virgin, so Jesus' birth came about not as a result of human love or lust, but through a remarkable life-giving operation of the Holy Spirit (Matthew 1:20; Luke 1:35). This may be difficult for us to understand because in human experience it is totally impossible. But in the birth of our Saviour, God was doing something special that was way beyond human thought or imagination.

Son of Man

The New Testament uses many titles and names for the Lord Jesus but the one he himself used most often was Son of Man. No one else addressed Jesus in this way: there must be something special in the title for Jesus to use it so often. By the use of this title Jesus made it plain that he really was a man. He was a unique man and a sinless man, but nevertheless he was truly man. This was crucial for our salvation. Listen to Hebrews 2:14-17.

- 'Since the children have flesh and blood, he too shared in their humanity so that by his death he might destroy him who holds the power of death — that is, the devil — and free those who all their lives were held in slavery by their fear of death. For surely it is not angels he helps, but Abraham's descendants. For this reason he had to be made like his brothers in every way, in order that he might become a merciful and faithful high priest in service to God, and that he might make atonement for the sins of the people.'

Jesus had to become a man in order to make atonement for man's sins. It was man who had broken God's law and sinned, therefore it had to be man who would pay the penalty for that sin. But there was no man qualified to do this, so God became man in the person of Jesus Christ and did for us what was crucial to our salvation.

Son of God

Jesus was more than a man. Twenty-five times in the Gospels he calls himself the Son of God. Jesus is Emmanuel, which means 'God with us'. It is true that God had always been with his people and we can see in the Old Testament that he was with Moses and David. However, in Jesus, God was with us in a very different way. In Jesus, God becomes man, takes to himself human nature and identifies himself with us in a way the Old Testament saints never experienced.

Jesus is truly man and truly God. He is not part man and part God. In him there exists two natures so that he is divine and also a sinless man. His deity is affirmed throughout Scripture. In the Old Testament the prophet Isaiah was given a remarkable revelation of the glory and holiness of God. He sees and hears the angelic host crying,

- 'Holy, holy, holy is the Lord Almighty; the whole earth is full of his glory' (Isaiah 6:3).

Isaiah himself says of this,

- 'My eyes have seen the King, the Lord Almighty' (v.5).

But in the New Testament, referring to this incident, the apostle John says,

- 'Isaiah said this because he saw Jesus' glory and spoke about him' (John 12:41).

Jesus, then, is the holy Lord of whom the angels spoke. Jesus is the King, the Lord Almighty, whom Isaiah saw. Jesus is God.

Jesus the Saviour

Salvation was planned in heaven but it could not be accomplished in heaven. Atonement for sin must be made to God by man's representative. But there was no man qualified to do this, for all men are sinners. The eternal God became man, 'so that by his death' (Hebrews 2:14) he might accomplish salvation for his people. God became man so that as the man Jesus he could die for his people and purchase their salvation. Paul puts it like this in Romans 5:17: 'For if, by the trespass of the one man [Adam], death reigned through that one man, how much more will those who receive God's abundant provision of grace and of the gift of righteousness reign in life through the one man, Jesus Christ.'

If we were to ask, 'What is God like?', the answer the Bible would give is that he is like Jesus — holy, righteous, good, full of compassion and mercy. He loves sinners and stretches out his arms in love and grace to them, calling upon them to come to him. The sinner's only hope of salvation rests on this great truth of who Jesus is, because God can only be known through the Lord Jesus Christ.

It's worth quoting

'You must make your choice. Either this man was, and is, the Son of God: or else a madman or something worse. You can shut him up for a fool; you can spit at him and kill him for a demon; or you can fall at his feet and call him Lord and God. But let us not come with any patronising nonsense about his being a great human teacher. He has not left that open to us. He did not intend to' (C. S. Lewis).

Think about it

1. Why is it important for Christians to defend vigorously the uniqueness and exclusiveness of Jesus?
2. Try and think through in your mind the amazing truth that Jesus is truly Man and truly God. Avoid trying to explain the facts and think on how crucial this is to your salvation.

Further reading

John Blanchard, *Will the real Jesus please stand up?*, Evangelical Press

5.
The Holy Spirit

It is not too difficult to think of God as the Father and God as the Son, but God the Holy Spirit presents us with a problem. It is easy to think of Father and Son as personalities but it is not so straightforward to think of God the Holy Spirit as a person. The tendency is to think of the Holy Spirit as a power or influence — an 'it' not a 'he'. This would be a fatal mistake because the Holy Spirit is as much God as the Father and Son.

We have already seen in Isaiah 6 and John 12 that 'the King, the Lord Almighty' whom the prophet saw was Jesus. The same Isaiah 6 passage is quoted again in Acts 28:26-27, and Paul says that the person speaking there was the Holy Spirit. Just as Jesus is God so also the Holy Spirit is God.

His ministry

The ministries of God the Father, God the Son and God the Holy Spirit are all essential for our salvation. The Father planned it, the Son purchased it and the Holy Spirit applies it to us. This he does, says Jesus, by giving us new life (John 3:5-8) and by convicting us of sin (John 16:8). Without conviction there can be no repentance and without repentance there can be no salvation.

The reason we need saving is the terrible hold that sin has on all of us. God's plan for our salvation did not break that power of sin; Jesus dying on the cross was crucial if that power was to be broken; but it was not enough. When God planned our salvation he knew of the awful power of sin over us, and he knew that if left to ourselves we would never come to Jesus for the salvation he died to purchase for us. Facing this problem in John 6:44 Jesus said, 'No one will come to me unless the Father who sent me draws him.'

God does this drawing by the ministry of the Holy Spirit. The Spirit uses the truth about Jesus in the gospel and through this he brings conviction of sin. Only the Holy Spirit can do this. Conviction is the knowledge of the reality of our own sin; it is to feel its awfulness; it is to grieve that our sin has offended God. Conviction brings a longing for salvation. It turns us to Jesus for forgiveness. All this is the work of the Holy Spirit in our hearts.

His fruit

After we are saved the Holy Spirit goes on working in us, seeking to produce in our lives his own special fruit — love, joy, peace, patience, kindness, goodness, faithfulness, gentleness and self-control (Galatians 5:22). This fruit is much more than temperamental traits that we may or may not have by nature. It should be seen in all Christians irrespective of what we are naturally like. Yet again, only the Holy Spirit can do this. These are spiritual qualities which are the result of a life submitted in loving obedience to the directions of the Holy Spirit as found in Scripture.

His gifts

In recent years there has been a great deal of controversy over the gifts of the Holy Spirit. Some Christians think that all the miraculous gifts we read of in the New Testament are available to the church today. Others believe that the gifts were withdrawn by God at the end of the apostolic age. A small book like this is not the place to argue the rights and wrongs of the case. But we must believe that without the enabling of the Holy Spirit we are useless in the work of the gospel. We need to know afresh an out-pouring of the Spirit's power on the church and this should be the urgent prayer of all believers.

It's *worth quoting*

'I think you will agree with me when I say that many people are confused about the Spirit of God. The Holy Spirit, for instance, is not enthusiasm. Some people get enthusiastic, and they imagine it is the Holy Spirit. Some who can get all worked up over a song imagine that this is the Spirit, but this does not necessarily follow. Some of these same people go out and live just like the sinful world — but the Holy Spirit never enters a man and then lets him live just like the world that God hates... The Holy Spirit must be Lord, or he will not come at all' (A. W. Tozer).

Think about it

1. What do you think is the relevance of the Isaiah 6 passage being quoted in John 12 and Acts 28?
2. How did the Holy Spirit draw you to Christ? What influences did he use that you can only appreciate now as you look back on your conversion?
3. Tozer said, 'The Holy Spirit must be Lord'. What does this mean and what are the evidences that he is Lord in your life?

Further reading

Sinclair Ferguson, *The Holy Spirit*, IVP

6.
The Trinity

The word 'trinity' is not found in the Bible but the idea it presents is seen everywhere in Scripture from the use of the plural 'us' in Genesis 1:26: 'Then God said, Let us make man in our image', to the baptismal formula of Matthew 28:19: 'baptizing them in the name of the Father and of the Son and of the Holy Spirit'. Trinity means 'threeness' and speaks of God as Father, Son and Holy Spirit. We do not believe in three Gods. Scripture is clear that there is only one God (Deuteronomy 6:4; 1 Timothy 2:5).

There is no doubt that this is a very difficult doctrine to understand. Augustine, one of the great Christian leaders of the fifth century, gave a great deal of time to thinking about the doctrine of the Trinity. One day, as he was walking along the seashore, he saw a boy digging in the sand. He asked him what he was trying to do, and the youngster replied that he wanted to empty the sea into his hole in the sand. This set Augustine thinking: 'Am I not trying to do the same thing as this child, in seeking to exhaust with my reason the infinity of God and to collect it within the limits of my own mind?'

One God — three persons

Christians have been accused, particularly by the followers of Islam, of worshipping three Gods, but, as we have
seen, that is not true. God is so great and glorious that it is
impossible, as Augustine discovered, for the mind of man
to grasp all that he is. Our minds are limited and in order
to try and explain the Trinity we have come up with vari-
ous illustrations of one substance in three forms — water,
ice and steam, or, the three leaves on a shamrock. These
may help, but not much, because there is nothing in human experience to compare with God in his Trinitarian
form.

The word 'person' does not help either. If we think of a
person, he will have his own identity and being, so three
persons will be three individuals. Language, even though
we must use it, cannot do justice to the majesty of God.
When it comes to God we are simply left with what he
chooses to tell us about himself in the Bible. There we find
God revealed as Father, Son and Holy Spirit — one God
in three persons.

The Trinity is not a matter for debate or even attempted
explanation, but for a reverent acceptance.

The Trinity at work

In the Trinity there is a certain order: first is the Father,
then the Son and then the Holy Spirit. Yet at the same

time the three persons are all God, equal with each other and as important as each other. One is no more superior than the other two but they have a different work or function. We can see this in God's works of creation and salvation.

In creation God is said to have created the heavens and earth (Genesis 1:1). But also we are told that he did this through the Son. And if we go back to Genesis 1:2 we see that the Holy Spirit was involved in creation hovering over the waters or bringing into existence what God had ordained. This would be in accord with Psalm 104:30: 'When you send your Spirit, they are created, and you renew the face of the earth.' So God the Father created the world and he did it through the Son and by the means of the Holy Spirit.

In salvation we can again see the whole Trinity at work. God the Father planned it. It was he who loved the world and out of this love sent Jesus the Son to be our Saviour. Without this initial act of the Father there would be no salvation. Jesus makes this very clear in John 6:37-38: 'All that the Father gives me will come to me, and whoever comes to me I will never drive away. For I have come down from heaven not to do my will but to do the will of him who sent me.'

God the Son died in our place on the cross. Jesus 'was delivered over to death for our sins and was raised to life for our justification' (Romans 4:25).

God the Holy Spirit makes all this real and applies to us the merits of Christ's death. Paul acknowledged that what saved the Christians at Corinth was not the persuasive words he preached but the Holy Spirit demonstrating divine power by using the message preached.

Peter brings all this together: 'To God's elect ... who have been chosen according to the foreknowledge of God the Father, through the sanctifying work of the Spirit, for obedience to Jesus Christ and sprinkling by his blood' (1 Peter 1:2).

It's *worth* quoting

'We are deeply conscious that the Trinity is a mystery beyond our comprehension. The glory of God is incomprehensible. There are no analogies for what we have been describing. There is no way we can picture this truth. You can have three men, each of whom is equally human, and distinct from the other. But at the end of the day you will have three men, and not one. The three persons of the Godhead are each equally God, and distinct from each other. The mystery is that you still have but one God' (Stuart Olyott).

Think about it

1. If the word 'person' does not help in our thinking about the Trinity, why do we use it?

2. As you consider the work of the Trinity in salvation,
   would it be possible for a sinner to be saved if any one
   of these three acts of God was missing?

Further reading

Stuart Olyott, *The Three are One*, Evangelical Press

7.
Sin
Breaking the law of God

We need to understand Genesis 3 if we are to understand the gospel. Everything else that follows in the Bible does so as a consequence of the events that took place in the Garden of Eden. And they were events, not myths. Underlying all the actions of Jesus and all the teaching of the New Testament is the fact of human sin and the doctrine of the fall of man. By the Fall we mean man's fall from the perfect condition in which he was created to a state of sin.

Our responsibility

Whilst it is clear from Genesis 3 that Satan is behind sin, this does not excuse us nor does it remove our responsibility for our actions. The words which the Bible later uses to describe human disobedience to God emphasize this.

- *Sin* means to fall short of the standard God has set.
- *Transgression* is to trespass outside the boundaries God has set.

- *Iniquity* means crookedness, not straight, moral distortion, and refers to our nature.

Read Psalm 32:1-2 NKJV, where all three words are used.

The three words tell us that we have gone against the will of God. Our crooked and twisted nature refuses to stay inside God's boundaries and leaves us well short of God's standard. It is our sin that causes the problem and we are answerable for it. It is not environment or upbringing or parents or lack of privileges, it is our fault and God holds us responsible. There is no escaping that.

God's wrath

God's wrath is his anger against those who sin and his determination to punish them. It is divine holiness stirred into action against violations of his holy law. God, who is utterly and completely holy, cannot regard evil and good as the same. He cannot smile benevolently upon both truth and lies. So God's holiness makes hell as inevitable as his love makes heaven.

God never excuses sin. This is actually proved beyond all doubt by the cross of Jesus. On the cross sin is punished and borne by our substitute, the Lord Jesus Christ. No sin is excusable, but, thank God, it is pardonable in Christ. God's wrath is as real as his love, but it is not like human wrath. It is not vindictive, capricious or irrational.

It is a right and necessary reaction against moral evil. It is judicial wrath against guilty sinners: God is only angry when anger is called for.

Sin's reality today

In Romans 1 Paul exposes the sin of his day but the words there could well be describing today's society.

v.21	There is an almost total rejection of God.
v.22	Men are wise enough to put men on the moon but foolish enough for all the violence, wars and crime of today.
v.23	God is openly dishonoured as God and Jesus are made the subject of laughter and scorn.
v.24	Men and women degrade their bodies with sex, drink and drugs.
vv.26-27	Rampant homosexuality and lesbianism are as blatant today as they were in Sodom.
v.28	In nations that were built upon the Christian ethic, the knowledge and law of God are no longer retained and all sorts of laws are passed to legalize what God forbids.

It's *worth quoting*

'Much that we take for granted in a civilized society is based upon the assumption of human sin. Nearly all legislation has grown up because human beings cannot be trusted to settle their own disputes with justice and without self-interest. A promise is not enough; we need a contract. Doors are not enough; we have to lock and bolt them. The payment of fares is not enough; tickets have to be issued, inspected and collected. Law and order are not enough; we need the police to enforce them. All this is due to man's sin. We cannot trust each other. We need protection against one another. It is a terrible indictment of human nature' (John Stott).

Think about it

1. In Genesis 3 when Adam sinned he lost certain blessings. What were they?

   Verse 7: ....
   Verses 8-10: ....
   Verses 14-15: ....

2. We have paraphrased Romans 1:21-28 in this chapter but to catch the full significance of the passage, write it out from your Bible.

Further reading

Robert Murray M'Cheyne, *Conviction of sin,* Evangelical Press

8.

Atonement
God dealing with sin

The doctrine of atonement is the biblical teaching on the meaning of the death of the Lord Jesus Christ. The atonement is God's answer to human sin, and, as such, is the only effective answer to our sinfulness and guilt. It is crucial therefore that we have a full biblical understanding of what it means.

God's way of salvation did not start in the New Testament when Jesus came into the world. In the Old Testament God ordained certain events that, though important in the lives of the Israelite people at the time, were even more important as vivid illustrations of what Jesus Christ was going to accomplish when he came into the world.

The Old Testament pictures remind us of two basic facts about the atonement. First, it was planned by God. Peter refers to the death of Jesus as being, 'by God's set purpose and foreknowledge' (Acts 2:23). He later says that Jesus 'was chosen before the creation of the world' to shed his blood for us (1 Peter 1:20). God planned it all to demonstrate his love for us (Romans 5:8). Secondly, there is nothing hit or miss about our salvation. The death of Jesus was not a tragic mistake but 'God's set purpose'. All the events that led up to Calvary were under God's control. When Pilate said to Jesus that he had power to free him or crucify him, Jesus replied, 'You would have no power over me if it were not given to you from above' (John 19:11). God was in charge at Calvary not Pilate.

The supreme purpose of the Old Testament is to tell us about Christ and his cross. God even sent two of the great Old Testament leaders, Moses and Elijah, to speak to Jesus about the fulfilment of the prophecies dealing with his death (Luke 9:31).

Old Testament pictures

There are many Old Testament pictures that find their fulfilment in the death of Jesus, but perhaps the two most important are the Passover and the Day of Atonement.

The story of the Passover in Exodus 12 illustrates that the shed blood of the lamb saved God's people from his judgement of death. God promised them, 'When I see the blood, I will pass over you'; that is, 'My judgement will not touch you' (v.13). Paul likened the death of Jesus to this by describing Christ as our Passover Lamb (1 Corinthians 5:7).

The Day of Atonement in Leviticus 16 is a beautiful picture of the meaning of the death of Jesus. Hebrews chapters 9 and 10 are thrilling reading as they apply it to the cross of our Saviour.

Several things took place on the Day of Atonement but let us concentrate on the two goats mentioned in Leviticus 16:7-10. One was killed and its blood was taken by the high priest into the Most Holy Place and sprinkled on the mercy seat. This symbolized the turning away of the wrath of God from man's guilt. Mercy, instead of judgement, came to the sinner. The other goat, called the scapegoat, was brought to the high priest who laid his hands on the animal's head and confessed the sin of the people. Symbolically the sins were transferred to the scapegoat and it was sent into the desert, portraying the taking away of the sin of the people.

All this was symbolic. They were, says Hebrews 9:10, 'external regulations applying until the time of the new order'. That new order came with the Lord Jesus Christ. The death of our Saviour is the only sacrifice that God now recognizes. When Jesus died on the cross he did what both goats symbolized: he turned away the wrath of God from us and he took away our sin.

These pictures bring some important truths about the atonement sharply into focus. When Jesus died it was an act of substitution and propitiation.

Substitution

In the communion service (1 Corinthians 11:23-26) we are told the body of Jesus was broken *for you,* and his blood shed *for you.* These two little words are of enormous importance in understanding the atonement. They tell us that Jesus died in our place. He became our Substitute. He is the Passover Lamb, the Scapegoat, and the innocent victim who dies in the place of the guilty.

Propitiation

The propitiation means that on the cross, bearing our sin and guilt, Jesus faced the wrath of God instead of us, and fully paid on our behalf the debt we owed to the broken law of God. At Calvary Jesus made it possible for a holy God to be propitious — or favourably inclined — towards us, even though we are guilty sinners. God dealt with the problem of sin in the only way that could satisfy his holy justice and enable him to save a people who deserved only judgement.

Blood

Another word the Old Testament pictures keep bringing before us is the word blood. This word is vital to a true biblical understanding of the atonement. The New Testament writers keep telling us that we are saved by the blood of Jesus (Acts 20:28; Romans 3:25; 1 Peter 1:19; 1 John 1:7). They are describing the death of Jesus in the language of the Old Testament sacrifices, and the point they are making is that it is not merely the death of Jesus that atones for sin, but his sacrificial death. He did not die of natural causes or of an accident, but Jesus died as a sacrifice for our sin.

It's *worth quoting*

'Atonement is one of the difficult words in Scripture. It is found chiefly in the Old Testament and stands for the idea of "covering". Sin is thus said to be covered, or atoned for, by the Old Testament sacrifices described in Exodus and Leviticus. These sacrifices were designed symbolically to make amends for sin, and they pointed towards the effects of the work of Christ. The claims of God's holy law were satisfied by the Lord Jesus Christ. First in his life of obedience, and then in his suffering of the wages of sin in his own body on the tree, and so he made an atonement for man's sin' (E. F. Kevan).

Think about it

1. In his hymn ' Not all the blood of beasts', Isaac Watts writes:

   My faith would lay her hand,
   On that dear head of thine,
   While like a penitent I stand,
   And there confess my sin.

   Look up the hymn in your hymn-book.

   What does this have to do with the scapegoat?

2. Look up Luke 9:31.
    What do you think Moses and Elijah spoke about with
    Jesus?
    What was about to be fulfilled in Jerusalem?

Further reading

Tom Wells, *A price for a people,* Banner of Truth Trust

9.
Grace
God's mercy to the undeserving

The grace of God is the most thrilling concept that can occupy the mind of a Christian, and when it occupies the mind it will soon flood the heart with praise to God that such a thing exists. Without grace there is no hope for any of us. The only alternative to grace is salvation by our own efforts. This is a non-starter because God will not accept it. The New Testament makes that abundantly clear.

- 'Therefore no one will be declared righteous in his sight by observing the law; rather, through the law we become conscious of sin' (Romans 3:20).
- 'For it is by grace you have been saved, through faith — and this not from yourselves, it is the gift of God — not by works, so that no one can boast' (Ephesians 2:8-9).
- 'He saved us, not because of righteous things we had done, but because of his mercy' (Titus 3:5).

If salvation is to be effective it has to be acceptable to God. This is why grace is the key word in the gospel, because it delights in the Lord Jesus Christ as the sacrifice which God himself has provided. If we do not understand the New Testament meaning of the word grace, we will never understand the gospel, because grace is the key to understanding the substance and heart of its message, which is salvation through Christ alone.

- God is a God of grace (1 Peter 5:10)
- Jesus brings grace to the world (John 1:17)
- The Holy Spirit is a Spirit of grace (Hebrews 10:29)
- Salvation is a product of grace (Titus 2:11)
- Justification is by grace (Romans 3:24)
- Redemption is according to grace (Ephesians 1:7)

What is grace?

Grace is needed because of both the character of man and the character of God. Though man was created in the image of God, able to know and enjoy him, when man sinned he was separated from God, and sin has since domi- nated all his actions. He is now alien to God his Maker and, because of his sinful character, he can do nothing about it. God's character on the other hand is such that he cannot condone or overlook sin. His holiness, truth and justice demand that man must be dealt with as he is, and that sin must be punished.

These two factors, taken on their own, would condemn all men to an eternity in hell. But God's character is also such that, though he hates sin, he loves the guilty sinner who deserves his judgement. Divine love therefore plans salvation, and divine grace provides salvation. Grace is the free, unmerited, undeserved favour of God to sinners.

How grace works

In Ephesians 2:4-5 we find three great gospel words — love, mercy and grace. Out of God's love and mercy flows grace. Grace is not some abstract idea; it is God working. Grace is God loving the unlovely, pardoning the guilty and saving the lost. Grace is the unique work of God. We do not deserve grace because our sin is our own fault. What we deserve is hell, but in Christ we receive grace and every blessing and benefit that flows from it. Salvation by grace is an eternal salvation. It depends upon the merit of Christ, not our merit; therefore it never fails or loses its power.

It's *worth quoting*

'Salvation is not in any sense God's response to anything in us. It is not something that we in any sense deserve or merit. The whole essence of the teaching at this point, and everywhere in all the New Testament, is that we have no sort or kind of right whatsoever to salvation, that the whole glory of salvation is that though we deserve nothing but punishment and hell and banishment out of the sight of God to all eternity, yet God, of his own love and grace and wondrous mercy, has granted us this salvation. Now this is the entire meaning of this term grace' (D. M. Lloyd-Jones).

Think about it

1. Why should the believer thank God every day that salvation is by grace alone?
2. Why will God not accept a salvation based on our own efforts? Do you think there would be more people in heaven if salvation was gained by human effort?
3. Salvation by works or self-help has always been a popular belief. How could you persuade someone that it is wrong?

Further reading

D. M. Lloyd-Jones, *The Cross*, Kingsway

10.
Regeneration
A new spiritual birth

When Jesus told Nicodemus, 'You must be born again' (John 3:7), he was speaking of the need for regeneration.

The gospel addresses itself to sinners who are dead in sin (Ephesians 2:1). ' Dead' is a very strong word. There are no degrees of deadness. You cannot be half dead. If you are dead you are totally unable to do anything to change your condition (Jeremiah 13:23). A dead man in a coffin can do absolutely nothing to prevent a burial. When Paul says we are dead in sin, he means we are unable to change our spiritual condition. We are spiritually helpless and hopeless and if our condition is to change, God must do it because we cannot. We need to be born again.

Regeneration precedes everything

Regeneration is not the same as conversion, no more than justification is exactly the same as redemption. The great New Testament words of salvation all have a different emphasis to make and they teach us that there are different steps in salvation. These steps must start somewhere and regeneration is the place where the work of grace begins in the sinner.

To repent and to believe are things that God demands we do. They are our response to the gospel. But we cannot do them if we are dead in sin. In order to be able to respond to spiritual truths we must have spiritual life in us, we must be born again. This precedes everything and is the work of God alone. It has to be. So being born again is the initial step in salvation. Jesus is telling us that man in sin does not need patching up with religion or morality or education. He needs a complete new beginning. Man had a beginning once in Adam. That was good but it was ruined by sin.

We need to be born again and given an ability again to respond to God. This is exactly what the gospel offers us and only the gospel can do this. Sometimes you hear of a man making a new start in life. He changes his home and his job and says he is having a new start. But he is not. He is changing many things but he cannot change his nature. Spiritual new birth gives the sinner a new start with a new nature, a new heart (Ezekiel 36:26-27). This can only be done by God.

Spiritual birth

The new birth is a spiritual birth, it is not a physical birth as Nicodemus seemed to think in John 3:4. Yet it is interesting to parallel the two types of birth, for the physical illustrates the spiritual. For instance, in our physical birth we contribute nothing. It is a result of a process initiated by our parents. So too is the spiritual birth; it is initiated by God our heavenly Father. Without a physical birth we could have no physical existence; so too without a spiritual birth we have no spiritual life. Man is born in sin with a nature already alien to God. We are spiritually dead. New birth gives us a spiritual existence.

A necessity

When Jesus told Nicodemus he must be born again, he was speaking to a very religious man. Often religious people say that they can see that criminals and drug addicts and people like that need a new beginning because of the mess they have made of their lives. But they, themselves, are not like that. They are honest, industrious, respectable, therefore they do not need to be born again. But as far as Jesus is concerned there are no exceptions to this. Without this spiritual birth there is no spiritual life. There can be religious life and moral life but there will be no spiritual life.

It is the work of the Holy Spirit to regenerate us. This he does by bringing sinners under the sound of the gospel. 'Faith comes through hearing the message' (Romans 10:17). Through the gospel message the Holy Spirit shows us our true condition. All have sinned, the good respectable people and the moral outcasts. The Spirit convinces us that we need to be born again, and then brings us in repentance and faith to Christ.

It's worth quoting

'Regeneration is the beginning of all saving grace in us, and all saving grace in exercise on our part proceeds from the fountain of regeneration. We are not born again by faith or repentance or conversion; we repent and believe because we have been regenerated' (John Murray).

Think about it

1. When it comes to the human spiritual condition, how dead is dead?
2. What is the difference between religious and moral life, and spiritual life?
3. If regeneration precedes everything in salvation, does this mean that the sinner is not responsible for refusing to believe the gospel?

Further reading

Peter Jeffery, *From Religion to Christ*, Calvary Press

II.

Repentance and faith
Turning from sin to God

Where there is true faith there will inevitably be repentance. Sometimes it is asked, which comes first; this is a
pointless question because they are interdependent. Faith
and repentance cannot exist without one another.

Repentance has two sides; it is a turning from sin and
to God (Acts 3:19). For true repentance both these elements
are essential. A man can turn from sin without turning to
God. He may see the value of changing his lifestyle and
decide to refrain from certain bad habits. No doubt this
will do him good in many ways, but spiritually it will be
useless. On the other hand, a man may turn to God and
cry for mercy, but have no intention of leaving his sin. His
eyes may be wet with tears and his heart as hard as stone.

True repentance involves seeing sin for what it really is;
not just a character defect, but a permanent attitude of
rebellion against the love and care and righteous authority
of God. It is this new understanding of God and of one's
own sin that leads to true repentance. There will also be a
great desire to break with the past and to live in future only
to please God (Acts 26:20). That is repentance.

Faith is an unwavering trust in the Lord Jesus Christ as
the only Saviour to deal with sin (Acts 20:21; Romans

3:25). It is not merely an intellectual assent to a set of doctrines, but a coming to Christ in repentance, crying for mercy. Faith hears the truth of the gospel, believes it and then acts upon it. Saving faith progresses from a belief in certain facts to a real trusting in Christ and what he has done on our behalf and for our salvation. Faith is a response of the mind and heart to the Saviour of whom the gospel speaks (1 Peter 1:21).

Ongoing repentance

Repentance does not stop when we are saved. After regeneration we are still sinners and sadly we still break the law of God. The Christian life is a continual battle with sin therefore repentance has to be a daily experience. In fact it is often the case that the believer knows a deeper conviction of sin and a deeper sense of repentance after conversion than he did before. David's prayer of repentance in Psalm 51 is an example of this.

We are to repent every day for the sin of that day. Sin that is not confessed and repented of will fester in our hearts and destroy our fellowship with God.

It's *worth quoting*

'True faith is not passive but active. It requires that we meet certain conditions, that we allow the teachings of Christ to dominate our total lives from the moment we believe. The man of saving faith must be willing to be different from others. The effort to enjoy the benefits of redemption while enmeshed in the world is futile. We must choose one or the other; and faith quickly makes its choice, one from which there is no retreat' (A. W. Tozer).

Think about it

1. If a man says he has faith in Christ but has never repented of his sin and turned to God, is that a genuine biblical faith?
2. Why are the two sides of repentance absolutely necessary?
3. David's repentance in Psalm 51 is that of a believer. Why is it that a Christian should need such a depth of repentance? Would not the fact that he can never lose his salvation make this unnecessary?

Further reading

Peter Jeffery, *The Young Spurgeon*, Evangelical Press

12.
Reconciliation
Removing the hostility of sin

The Bible says that man is a slave to sin and because of that sin he is an enemy of God. Sin gives rise to hostility between the holy God and sinful man. It creates a massive barrier that we would be incapable of removing, even if we wanted to.

God's answer to this is reconciliation, which means to bring together two persons by removing the hostility that had previously existed between them. On four occasions the New Testament speaks of the work and ministry of Christ in terms of reconciliation: Romans 5:10; 2 Corinthians 5:18-21; Ephesians 2:16; Colossians 1:22.

In each of these passages the hostility between God and man is stressed. They are enemies and alienated, and therefore need reconciling.

Let's look at 2 Corinthians 5:18-21 in detail and see that reconciliation is described in four simple steps.

'God was reconciling the world to himself in Christ, not counting men's sin against them…Be reconciled to God. God made him who had no sin to be sin for us, so that in him we might become the righteousness of God.'

1.   God does not count our sin against us.

Our sin is our responsibility so we should bear its consequences. Each sin is like an individual item on a bill and
every time we sin the debt grows. But in reconciliation
God wipes the slate clean; he removes every debt on the
bill, thus leaving us with nothing to pay. He does not count
our sin against us either now or in the future.

But what happens to our sins? Are they just forgotten?
No, God cannot do that. These sins have to be answered
for. The debt has to be paid in full and God's holy law has
to be satisfied. If God does not count our sins against us,
what does he do with them?

2.   He counts our sins against Christ.

God makes Jesus responsible for our sin. Jesus willingly
accepts that terrible responsibility and God lays on him
the sin and guilt of his people.

3.   Christ bears the punishment that was due to us.

Jesus, now bearing our sin, is treated by God as we deserve to be treated and the full wrath of God falls upon
our sin-bearer on the cross. Sin, which is the barrier, is
dealt with legally and decisively.

4.   God credits the righteousness of Jesus to us.

The last stage in reconciliation is that, having dealt with
our sin in Christ, God now counts to us the righteousness

of his Son and he is now able to treat us as he would normally treat the Lord Jesus. The barrier between God and man has been dealt with and reconciliation is accomplished.

It's *worth quoting*

'Reconciliation means the ending of enmity and the making of peace and friendship between persons previously opposed. God and men were at enmity with each other by reason of men's sins; but God has acted in Christ to reconcile sinners to himself through the cross. The achieving of reconciliation was a task which Christ completed at Calvary. In virtue of Christ's finished work of atonement, God now invites sinners everywhere to receive the reconciliation and thus be reconciled to him. Believers enjoy through Christ an actual reconcilement with God which is perfect and final' (J. I. Packer).

Think about it

1. Romans 5:10 says we are reconciled through
   ....
   Ephesians 2:16 says it's through ....
   Colossians 1:22 through ....

   Are these different means of reconciliation or are they all the same?

2. In 2 Corinthians 5, reconciliation is possible because God did not count our sins against us. Is this saying the same thing as the other three verses?
3. In your own words describe the message of reconciliation.

Further reading

J. C. Ryle, *Thoughts for young men,* Calvary Press

13.
Redemption
Set free from the bondage of sin

We have seen that the Bible says that man is dead in sin. Another way Scripture describes man's spiritual condition is that he is in bondage or slavery to sin (Romans 6:20; 2 Peter 2:19). Just as the man who is spiritually dead needs regenerating, so the same man who is also a slave to sin needs redeeming. Redemption means to set free from the slavery of sin by the payment of a ransom price.

Slavery to sin

If man was spiritually free there would be no need of redemption; but the slavery to sin is real. It is not an illusion but the common fact about every human being. Sin is a great deceiver. It holds before us endless pleasures but fails to tell of the price or consequence of following its attractions. In Genesis 3 the awful reality of sin is shown to us. Then in the next chapter we see the effects of sin as a man kills his brother. By the time we get to Genesis 6 sin's dominance is seen in every human being: 'every inclination of the thoughts of his heart was only evil all the time' (v. 5).

In the New Testament the power of sin comes to its terrible climax when men kill the Son of God. From then on, the New Testament spells out sin's consequences in frightening clarity in passages like Romans 1:18-32. In Romans 7 Paul puts into words the experience of every man and woman: 'We know that the law is spiritual; but I am unspiritual, sold as a slave to sin. I do not understand what I do. For what I want to do I do not do, but what I hate I do' (vv. 14-15).

It is from this bondage that Jesus came to redeem us.

The Redeemer

Jesus has paid the ransom price that can set sinners free from the bondage of sin and he has paid the price once and for all. Christ redeems us from:

- All wickedness (Titus 2:14)
- The grip of sin (Romans 6:18,22)
- The curse of the law (Galatians 3:13)
- The bondage of the law (Galatians 4:5)
- Death (Job 5:20)
- Hell (Psalm 49:15)

Redemption means to buy out of slavery, but the purchase price to set us free from sin is enormous. The price is way beyond anything we could afford. This is why Peter says that we are not redeemed with silver or gold but with the precious blood of the Lamb of God (1 Peter 1:18-19). Only Jesus could pay that price.

The ransom price

Jesus told us that the reason he came into the world was 'to give his life as a ransom for many' (Mark 10:45). The word ransom is familiar to us when we read of someone who has been kidnapped and a ransom price is demanded to set him free. Jesus teaches us that his death is the means by which we are set free. He gave his life as the price of freedom for the slaves of sin. Redemption is a costly business. Peter has reminded us of that, and so too does Paul: 'In him we have redemption through his blood, the forgiveness of sins, in accordance with the riches of God's grace' (Ephesians 1:7).

The ransom price is the blood of Jesus, or, in other words, his sacrificial death on the cross. We are not redeemed by the teaching of Jesus or by the fact that he could do miracles. It is what he did on the cross that purchased our salvation.

We are not to think that the ransom price was paid to Satan as if he had some right to the payment. It is true we were the slaves of sin, but Satan's power was that of an invader or usurper. He had no rights of ownership. It was God who made us and all the rights are his. So the ransom price was paid to satisfy the demands of God's law which we had violated by our sin. The law demanded that the wage of sin be the death of the sinner. Christ satisfied that demand on behalf of his people when he shed his blood on the cross. He took full responsibility for our sin. This included its guilt and punishment, and his death is the only payment that is acceptable to God.

It's worth quoting

'We were created for intimate fellowship with God and for freedom, but we have disgraced ourselves by unfaithfulness. First we have flirted with and then committed adultery with this sinful world and its values. The world has even bid for our soul, offering sex, money, fame, power and all the other items in which it traffics. But Jesus, our faithful bridegroom and lover, entered the market-place to buy us back. He bid his own blood. There is no higher bid than that. And we became his. He reclothed us, not in the wretched rags of our old unrighteousness, but in his new robes of righteousness' (James Montgomery Boice).

Think about it

1. How did you feel when you first realized you were in slavery to sin?
2. Galatians 3:13 says we are redeemed from the curse of the law. What is this curse? Find your answer by looking up the two Old Testament verses quoted by Paul in verses 10 and 13 (Deuteronomy 27:26 and 21:23).

Further reading

John Stott, *Basic Christianity*, IVP

14.
Justification
Made acceptable to God

Justification is the sovereign work of God in which he declares the guilty sinner to be righteous and the rightful demands of the law to be satisfied.

Takes away condemnation

Justification is the opposite of condemnation. We are condemned by God because of our sin (John 3:18-20) and if we were to appear before his throne of judgement he would have to find us guilty and sentence us to an eternity in hell. That would be a correct and legal verdict. In justification God the judge pronounces us acquitted of the charge. He does not say we are innocent because we are not, but we are acquitted. We are not condemned but declared to be acceptable to the holy God. Bearing in mind our guilt and that we deserve hell, this has to be the supreme demonstration of God's love and grace.

How can God do this? If we are guilty, how can he pronounce us to be pardoned? Does he bend the law?

Does he turn a blind eye to our sin? Does he forget all the declarations of judgement he has made upon sin? He does none of these things. He cannot ignore sin and still be a holy God. If God is to justify us he must do it in a way that makes sure he remains just and holy. How God does this we are told in Romans 3:21-26. That passage finishes with the words that God is 'just and the one who justifies the man who has faith in Christ'.

Gives us a righteousness

Justification does not only take away condemnation but gives to us a righteousness, and it is this righteousness that is the basis on which God now deals with us. This righteousness, says Romans 3:21, is 'apart from law'; that means that it is nothing to do with how we have kept the law of God. It is a righteousness from God — something that God gives us. In fact, it is Christ's righteousness. God credits us with the righteousness of his sinless Son. This is a staggering truth and it is the heart of the Christian gospel.

Our own righteousness is like filthy rags in God's sight (Isaiah 64:6). If we are to be acceptable to God we need something better than that. In Philippians 3:9 Paul delights that now that he is a Christian he has found 'the righteousness that comes from God and is by faith'. Isaiah expresses the same joy as Paul when he says, 'I delight greatly in the Lord; my soul rejoices in my God. For he has clothed me with garments of salvation and arrayed me in a robe of righteousness' (Isaiah 61:10).

How justification works

Romans 3 gives us the answer as to how justification works.

- It comes to us through faith (v.22)
- It is a product of God's grace (v.24)
- It is a result of all that Christ has done for us
  - He has redeemed us (v.24)
  - He was our propitiation (sacrifice for sin) (v.25)

In giving his Son to die in our place God demonstrated his justice. Our sins are not overlooked. They are dealt with exactly as God had always said they should be dealt with. They are punished, but because they had been laid on Jesus and he has taken responsibility for them, he takes our punishment instead of us. On the grounds of what Jesus has done, God is able to justify guilty sinners. He is acting in a perfectly lawful way because our sins have been dealt with according to divine law.

Our sins are credited to Jesus and God treats Jesus as he should treat us — he is forsaken and dies in our place. Jesus' righteousness is credited to us and God treats us as he has always treated Jesus — we become his children and he owns us as his redeemed people.

It's *worth quoting*

'It does not mean that we are made righteous, but rather that God regards us as righteous and declares us to be righteous. This has often been a difficulty to many people. They say that because they are conscious of sin within they cannot be in a justified state; but anyone who speaks like that shows immediately that he has no understanding of this great and crucial doctrine of justification. Justification makes no actual change in us; but is a declaration by God concerning us. It is not something that results from what we do but rather something that is done for us. We have only been made righteous in the sense that God regards us as righteous, and pronounces us to be righteous' (D. M. Lloyd-Jones).

Think about it

If salvation is not dependent upon us but is by grace alone through faith in Christ, does it matter how we live as Christians? Can we go on sinning as if it does not matter? Before you give an answer, read Romans 3:18.

Further reading

Joe Nesom, *Be sure what you believe* (Chapter 11, 'Innocent before God'), Evangelical Press

15.
Adoption

One of the great failures of modern non-biblical theology is its tendency to be unable to recognize the enormous barrier sin has erected between God and man. It therefore has no problem in proclaiming that God is the father of all men and women and consequently that we are all God's children. Jesus flatly contradicts this in John 8:42-47: 'If God were your Father, you would love me, for I am from God and now am here. I have not come on my own; but he sent me. Why is my language not clear to you? Because you are unable to hear what I say. You belong to your father, the devil...He who belongs to God hears what God says. The reason you do not hear is that you do not belong to God.'

In order to become a child of God a sinner has first of all to be justified. Based on justification the sinner can then be adopted into God's family (Ephesians 1:5; Galatians 4:4-5). Adoption is a term that Paul borrows from the first-century Roman legal system. In this system of law the adopted person was given the right to the name and property of the person who had adopted him. From a position of not belonging and having no rights he became a son with a father. His relationship and standing was changed and this change was brought about at the instigation of the adopting father. We can understand this clearly in the adoption process of our own legal system.

God's will

In Ephesians 1:4-5 Paul teaches that our spiritual adoption is based upon the love of God, the choice of God and the predestinating grace of God. God's love for us must have been very great to cause him to want to adopt such wilful, rebellious creatures as we are. Remember he was adopting the devil's children. There was nothing good in us that may have earned us the privilege of adoption, and anyway the predestinating and choosing was done before the creation of the world.

God's purpose in all this is that we should be holy and blameless. Such a condition would be impossible because of our sinful nature, but in the salvation we have in Christ, God changes our relationship to him in adoption, and in the sanctifying work of the Holy Spirit he begins to change our moral nature. God wants his adopted children to reflect his character and live according to his ways and laws.

Our privilege

Adoption conveys upon us all that sin makes impossible for us. Aliens become sons, strangers become children and enemies inherit all the blessings of God. In other words our relationship to God has totally changed, and it is no small change. To be a child of God makes us 'heirs of God and co-heirs with Christ' (Romans 8:17). To know that we will share in Christ's glory is a staggering thought. We, with all our pedigree of sin, are elevated to such a place of honour and privilege.

The world has nothing to compare with this. There is no more privileged person than a Christian. If we but realize what it means to be a child of God, our groans and complaints would disappear. Our expectation of tasting the good things of God would be greater and we would begin to live in accordance with our new standing of being adopted into the family of God.

> My God is reconciled,
> His pardoning voice I hear;
> He owns me for his child,
> I can no longer fear;
> With confidence I now draw nigh,
> And Father, Abba, Father! cry.

It's worth quoting

'Justification is the basic blessing on which adoption is founded; adoption is the crowning blessing, to which justification clears the way. Adopted status belongs to all who receive Christ (John 1:12). The adopted status of believers means that in and through Christ God loves them as

he loves his only begotten Son and will share with them all
the glory that is Christ's now (Romans 8:17, 38-39)' (J. I.
Packer).

Think about it

1. What is the relationship between justification and
   adoption?
2. Is God's purpose that we should be holy and blameless, too ambitious? How can those who were the children of the devil ever be holy?
3. Why is it important that our relationship to God should
   change?

Further reading

D. M. Lloyd-Jones, *The Sons of God (Romans 8:5-17),*
Banner of Truth Trust

16.
Union with Christ

Being a Christian is not just a matter of believing a set of doctrines. Of course belief and faith are crucial but the purpose of the work of salvation is to unite us with Christ. This is the heart of what it means to be a Christian. There is a living, vital, dynamic union with Christ that is not theoretical but real. This is why over 160 times in the New Testament Paul uses the words 'in him' or 'in Christ' or 'in Christ Jesus'.

For instance, in Christ . . .

- We have every spiritual blessing (Ephesians 1:3)
- We are chosen (Ephesians 1:4)
- We are brought near to God (Ephesians 2:13)
- We are created anew (Ephesians 2:10)
- We are loved by God (Romans 8:39)
- We are all one (Galatians 3:28)

A Christian is someone who is in Christ. Spiritual life comes from union with Christ, not by simply knowing what the Bible says (James 2:19). This does not mean that the Scriptures are unimportant. They are the means by which we believe, a sword wielded by the very hand of God, that can piece the heart and bring us to Christ (Hebrews 4:12; 1 Peter 1:23). Nevertheless, as far as the Bible is concerned no one can be a Christian unless they are in Christ.

Romans chapter 5 teaches that all people are either 'in Adam' or 'in Christ'.

In Adam

'In Adam' means in our natural state, the state or condition we are born in. In that condition...

- Sin and death reign (Romans 5:17)
- We are under the condemnation of God (Romans 5:18)
- Our life is marked by disobedience to God (Romans 5:19)

God regarded Adam as our representative or head and what therefore happened to him affects us all. When we become Christians, Jesus becomes our head and God regards what is true of Christ as being true of us. To see the truth of this, read Romans 5:15-19 slowly and carefully.

In Christ

Understanding what it means to be 'in Christ' is crucial for the everyday business of living the Christian life.

The first thing that happened to us in our union with

Christ was that the old self was crucified with Christ
(Romans 6:6). The old self or the old man means all we
were in Adam — rebellious, disobedient and sinful. All we
were in Adam was nailed to the cross. That's done. It has
happened and the result is 'that the body of sin might be
done away with, that we should no longer be slaves to sin'
(Romans 6:6). This is an amazing statement and it is not
talking of something that one day may become true of us
but what is already true now.

It does not mean that the believer lives untroubled by
the possibility of sinning, but it does mean that the body
of the Christian — his eyes, heart, mind, hands etc.— is
no longer a body controlled by sin. We are no longer slaves
to sin. It can still tempt us but it cannot compel us. Sin is
not our master any longer because we are 'in Christ'. He is
now our Lord and Master. Paul then goes on to say 'we
are dead to sin' (6:11), and because of this he can issue
the first command in the epistle to the Romans, 'Therefore
do not let sin reign in your mortal body so that you obey
its evil desires' (6:12). Sin will only reign in us if we *let* it.

In Romans 6 Paul is not talking about isolated acts of
sin but about its rule and dominance. All believers from
time to time will fall into individual acts of sin but no believer should let sin dominate his life.

It's *worth quoting*

'The New Testament describes a Christian as someone who
is "in Christ". You were united to Christ in God's decree of
election, being "chosen in Christ before the foundation of

the world" (Ephesians 1:4). When Christ lived his perfect
life on earth, that life was reckoned by God to be *your* life
— that is the truth of justification, which was explained in
Romans 1-5. When Christ died, his death was reckoned
by God to be *your* death, so that God declares there is no
longer any death for you to die as the penalty for your sin.
This, too, is something that Paul told us in chapters 1-5. In
the same way, when Christ rose from the dead, his resurrection was reckoned by God to be *your* resurrection
(Ephesians 2:5). The whole of your salvation depends upon
the fact of your union with Christ' (Stuart Olyott).

Think about it

1. Can a person be 'in Christ', and it make no difference
   to his lifestyle?
2. From Romans 5:15-19, list what is true of a man 'in
   Adam', and a man 'in Christ'.

Further reading

Sinclair Ferguson, *Handle with Care,* Hodder & Stoughton

17.
Sanctification
Being made like Jesus

The Bible speaks of sanctification in two ways. Firstly, we have been sanctified, 'But you were washed, but you were sanctified, but you were justified in the name of the Lord Jesus and by the Spirit of our God' (1 Corinthians 6:11, NKJV). In this verse, and others, sanctification is something that has taken place when God set us apart for service to him. This sanctification is ours because we are saved, because we are in Christ (1 Corinthians 1:2).

Secondly, the Bible refers to sanctification as a process that involves a moral and spiritual change in us once we are saved. It is this aspect of sanctification that we will be dealing with in this chapter.

Justification makes us right with God. You could go to heaven the moment you are justified because you are clothed with Christ's righteousness and therefore acceptable to God. But God does not stop at justifying us. He immediately begins in us the process of change called sanctification. Justification freed us from the guilt of sin and its condemnation. The process of sanctification begins to free us from the power of sin and its rule in our life. In this process God wants to make us more and more like the

Lord Jesus Christ (1 Thessalonians 4:3-4, 7). In this verse
'learning to control' is not a one-off effort but a prolonged
experience.

No one attains to complete sanctification in this life
(1 John 1:8). Yet the Scriptures tell us that the saints in
heaven are completely free from the power of sin (Hebrews
12:23; Revelation 14:5). This means that our sanctification is completed either at death or immediately after. But
it starts the moment we are justified.

Sanctification is hard work!

The evidence that someone is saved is that his life is being
changed (Colossians 3:1-10). This means that the Holy
Spirit begins to change his thinking, attitudes, desires, likes
and dislikes. The Bible calls this sanctification and it is not
an extra we may or may not take on, but an absolute
necessity.

Justification is all of God: man plays no part in it. Sanctification is also the work of God but we are expected to
work at it. We are able to do this because we are justified.
But even as we battle with our sin, and grapple with issues
in our lives, we are totally dependent upon God, knowing
that we can do nothing of ourselves. This is the way we
work out our salvation with fear and trembling (Philippians
2:12). It is as we see more and more of God that we realize our sinfulness. In his strength, we work hard at dealing
with our sin, because we love him. This is hard work, but

the extent to which we work at it will determine how sanctified we are. This explains why some Christians are holier than others and it also explains how it is possible for a believer to backslide. Even though we are saved there remains in us much of the old sinful nature. We must not pander to it. It must be resisted and fought, and our new nature must be allowed to rule (Ephesians 4:20-32). It is as we do this that our lives are made better, holier and more Christlike, because sanctification affects every part of us.

- Understanding (Jeremiah 31:33-34)
- Will (Ezekiel 36:25-27)
- Passions (Galatians 5:24)
- Conscience (Hebrews 9:14)

Sanctification means that the power of sin is being overcome in us. Now that we are new creatures in Christ, sin has no authority over us. It has no power to make us obey it. This does not mean that sin does not bother the Christian. Of course it does, but because its absolute authority and reign have ceased we can now triumph over it. We are no longer slaves to sin, under its heel and dominion. We are enemies of sin and resisting its evil influences. This is not easy. It involves effort and determination, and it is only possible because 'we know that our old self was crucified with him [Christ], so that the body of sin might be rendered powerless, that we should no longer be slaves to sin' (Romans 6:6).

Children of light

Paul spells out the practical effects of sanctification in
Ephesians chapters 4 & 5. But they do not just happen.
That is why the Apostle's language in 4:17 is so strong:
'So I tell you this and insist on it in the Lord, that you must
no longer live as the Gentiles do'. In 5:8-10 he is equally
insistent: 'For you were once darkness, but now you are
light in the Lord. Live as children of light (for the fruit of
the light consists in all goodness, righteousness and truth)
and find out what pleases the Lord.'

To live as children of light means:

- No lying (v.25)
- Control your anger (v.26)
- Stop stealing (v.28)
- No unwholesome talk (v.29)
- Get rid of bitterness, rage, anger, brawling, slander,
  malice (v.31)
- The mark of your life is to be kindness and compas-
  sion (v.32)
- Not even a hint of sexual immorality in you (5:3)

The list goes on. It is not exhaustive but it gives us a good
idea of the sort of lives God expects us to live. It is not an
easy life but it is possible because the indwelling presence
of the Holy Spirit gives us the power to live for God's
glory.

It's worth quoting

'Sanctification is a thing for which every believer is responsible … I maintain that believers are eminently and pecu-
liarly responsible, and under a special obligation to live
holy lives. They are not as others, dead and blind and
unrenewed; they are alive unto God, and have light and
knowledge, and a new principle within them. Whose fault
is it if they are not holy, but their own? On whom can they
throw the blame if they are not sanctified, but themselves?
God, who has given them grace and a new heart, and a
new nature, has deprived them of all excuse if they do not
live for his praise. This is a point which is far too much
forgotten. A man who professes to be a true Christian,
while he sits still, content with a very low degree of sanctification (if indeed he has any at all), and coolly tells you
he "can do nothing", is a very pitiable sight and a very
ignorant man. Against this delusion let us watch and be on
our guard' (J. C. Ryle).

Think about it

Can you look back in your life and see evidence of a changed
life brought about by justification and sanctification?

Further reading

Peter Jeffery, *Walk Worthy*, Bryntirion Press

18.
Election

The subject of election and predestination is undoubtedly one of the most controversial among Christians. Some believers love and treasure it as the most thrilling and humbling of doctrines; other believers will not tolerate it at any price and regard it as totally wrong. Let us first of all define what the Bible means by election.

All men and women are sinners, all are guilty of breaking God's law, therefore all deserve judgement and hell. No one deserves salvation, but election is God saving by his grace some guilty sinners whom he has chosen.

The elect are no better than anyone else. They are not chosen because they deserve something. So they can never feel superior to any who are not elect. The non-elect only get what their sin deserves so they can never complain that they are being treated unfairly.

God is a sovereign God; that is, a God who rules, not merely taking an interest in his creation but actually governing it. The Bible teaches that this God, who neither slumbers nor sleeps, is at any given moment in full control of the affairs of the world. He reigns over it, not with his hands tied waiting for the co-operation and permission of men, but as the almighty God. It is not surprising therefore that such a God can predestine and elect. All through the Bible we find him doing so.

- God chose Abraham (Nehemiah 9:7)
- God chose Israel (Deuteronomy 7:7)
- God chose David (1 Kings 8:16)
- God chose the apostles (John 6:70)
- God chooses his people (John 15:16)

Election and salvation

Jesus did not come into the world merely to make salvation possible. He came to save. There is an enormous difference between making something possible and actually doing it. Election in salvation simply means that God saves specific individuals. Paul states very clearly in Ephesians 1:4: 'For he chose us in him before the creation of the world.'

In the light of such clear teaching, why do some Christians find so much difficulty in accepting this doctrine? They say that election is unfair; why should God choose some and not others. Then they go on to argue that election removes human responsibility; so if man is not saved, God cannot blame him. Neither of these arguments is new and we find Paul answering them in Romans 9. That chapter very clearly teaches the doctrine of election.

It is not unfair, Paul says, and God is not unjust, and he then quotes Exodus 33:19 to show the biblical answer to this: 'I will have mercy on whom I will have mercy, and I will have compassion on whom I will have compassion.' God does not punish anyone unjustly. We are all sinners by nature and therefore we all deserve God's wrath. But God in his mercy saves some and in his justice condemns others. Far from being unfair, election is an act of divine mercy.

The human responsibility objection is answered in verse 19. Such an objection springs from ignorance of the true relationship between God and man (v. 20). God is our Creator, and who are we to dismiss something so clearly declared by God, simply because it is not acceptable to our little minds?

Election and foreknowledge

Some Christians, appealing to Romans 8:29 and 1 Peter 1:2, argue that all that is meant by election is that God, because of his omniscience, foreknew who would believe. So it is not a case of God choosing people for salvation, but rather of him seeing in advance what people would do and merely acknowledging it.

In the Bible foreknowledge means foreordained. In Acts 2:23, for example, we are told the death of Jesus was by 'God's set purpose and foreknowledge'. This does not mean that God foresaw what would happen to Jesus on the cross, but that he planned it.

Election is one of the most thrilling and humbling truths in Scripture, and it provides us with the greatest possible incentive for evangelism. As we spread God's Word we know he will use the truth to bring his elect to himself.

It's worth quoting

'Were there no election, there would be no calling, and no conversions, and all evangelistic activity would fail. But as it is, we know, as we spread God's truth, that his word will not return to him void. He has sent it to be the means whereby he calls his elect, and it will prosper in the thing for which he has sent it' (J. I. Packer).

Think about it

1. What do you think of the following statement: 'Election is the strongest possible encouragement to evangelize'?
2. Do you think that human pride has any part in the rejection of this doctrine?

Further reading

J. I. Packer, *You know God is in control, don't you?*, Calvary Press

19.
Eternal security

Eternal security means that we can never lose our salvation. The Christian can backslide and so lose the joy and sense of reality of his salvation, but he can never fall from grace, that is, never lose his salvation. We are saved by Christ and kept by Christ and there can be no truth more reassuring than that.

We all know our weaknesses and how prone we are to sin. Because of this we may be tempted at times to wonder if we are Christians at all. Most of us have problems in this area and they are as real twenty years after conversion as they are in the first year. If we are to let our assurance of salvation depend upon our actions we would never have security. Our hope is in what Christ has done for us, not in what we do for him. This does not mean we are to be indifferent to personal sin as we saw in the chapter on sanctification.

Inevitable

If we rightly understand the New Testament doctrine of salvation, we shall see that eternal security is inevitable.

Salvation is much more than forgiveness of sin — thank
God it is that, but it is more than that. When we are saved,
we are also adopted into the family of God. Romans 8:15-
17 and Galatians 4:4-7 speak of this, and both passages
tell us that salvation makes us heirs of God. What are we
to inherit? Paul tells us in Romans 8:17 that we are to
'share in his glory'.

The apostle Paul goes on to show us the four great
links in the chain of salvation.

- *Predestination,* which leads to calling.
- *Calling,* which leads to justification.
- *Justification,* which leads to glorification.
- *Glorification* (Romans 8:30).

Each of these links is as strong and certain as the others. And because of this, Paul is able to declare with
absolute conviction that nothing can separate believers
from the love of God (verses 38-39). He is delighting in
the certainty of glorification, the certainty of going to
heaven.

Jesus teaches the same truth in John 10:28: 'I give them
eternal life, and they shall never perish; no one can snatch
them out of my hand.' The life which the Good Shepherd
gives to his sheep is 'eternal life'; and so, inevitably, 'they
shall never perish'. How can they, if they have eternal life?
In Christ they have an eternal security.

It's *worth quoting*

'To his own sheep, then, Jesus gives eternal life. In terms
of the sheep metaphor, Jesus has already said that he gives
them "life … to the full", abundant life (v.10); now he plainly
states that such life is his own eternal life, frequently "hid-
den" in the Gospel under the figures of water, bread, light,
good pasture. The consequence of his knowing his sheep,
and of his gift to them of eternal life, is that they shall
never perish. It could not be otherwise, if they have eternal life…To think otherwise would entail the conclusion
that Jesus had failed in the explicit assignment given him
by the Father, to preserve all those given to him. The ulti-
mate security of Jesus' sheep rests with the Good Shepherd' (D. A. Carson).

Think about it

Follow Christ's teaching in John 10. Jesus gives to his sheep
eternal life. What does eternal mean?

Because of this the sheep shall never perish. What does
never mean?

1. *No one* can snatch them out of God's hand. What
    does *no one* mean?
    Is it possible that Jesus meant no one except ourselves?
    Did he mean that we can jump out of God's hand if
    we want to?

2. We are held in the hand of a Father who is greater than all. In order to get us out of this hand God would have to be forced to let us go, but no one can force God because he is greater than all.

   Therefore we are eternally secure.

Further reading

John Bunyan, *Grace abounding,* Evangelical Press

20.
The Second Coming

The Second Coming of Christ into the world is mentioned 318 times in the New Testament. So this is a doctrine with plenty of biblical support, but at the same time it is a very controversial doctrine. One reason for this is that Scripture does not tell us when the Lord will return. Quite clearly, times and dates are avoided (1 Thessalonians 5:1); the coming will be sudden and unexpected.

When Christ comes again it will be a personal and physical coming. 'The Lord himself will come down from heaven' (1 Thessalonians 4:16). He will come 'in the same way you have seen him go into heaven' (Acts 1:11) — that is, bodily and physically.

Hebrews 9:28 contrasts our Lord's first and second coming. The first coming was to deal with our sin. This involved Jesus becoming a servant, a man. He had to humble himself. But in the Second Coming he will come to bring us salvation that is already accomplished. He will come in triumph as King of Kings and Lord of Lords.

Comfort

This doctrine should be a source of great comfort to the
Christian. Paul tells us to 'encourage each other' with this
truth (1 Thessalonians 4:18). For the child of God this world
will always be a battlefield. There will always be struggles,
pain and sorrow. But Paul tells us that we are to rejoice in
sufferings (Romans 5:3). If Paul had told us to put up with
them without too much grumbling, we could perhaps
understand. But how do we rejoice in affliction, illness,
pressures, difficulties and persecutions? The answer is that
this world is not all there is. Christ will come again for his
people and take us to be in heaven with him. In the light of
this Paul says, 'I consider that our present sufferings are
not worth comparing with the glory that will be revealed in
us' (Romans 8:18).

Differences

There are differences of opinion between believers on the
Second Coming as to what is meant by the thousand years
or millennium in Revelation 20. There are three views on
this.

The *post-millennialism* view holds that the Second Com-
ing of Christ will follow the millennium.
The *pre-millennialism* view holds that Christ's Second
Coming will precede the millennium.

The a-*millennialism* or *non-millennialism* view holds that the thousand years of Revelation 20 is not to be understood literally, and there will be no actual millennium.

Some of the church's greatest Bible teachers have held different views on the Second Coming. For instance, Charles Hodge and Jonathan Edwards were post-millennialists; J. C. Ryle and Francis Schaeffer were pre-millennialists; and William Hendriksen and Dr Martyn Lloyd-Jones held to a-millennialism. The fact that such great men could differ on this doctrine should cause the rest of us to be cautious, and be aware of opposing too vigorously fellow believers who do not hold our viewpoint. Perhaps the most helpful comment on this matter is that made by Augustine. 'He who loves the coming of the Lord is not he who affirms that it is far off, nor is it he who says it is near, but rather he who, whether it be far off or near, awaits it with sincere faith, steadfast hope, and fervent love.'

It's *worth quoting*

'One of the notable elements in Peter's letters is the way in which he frequently points his readers forward to the life to come. His mind is full of the return of Christ, the Day of Judgement and the glory of heaven, and this perspective influences his writings profoundly.

'Why is he so interested in the future? Why does this pastor direct the eyes of his flock with such persistence to the last things? Is he a prophecy addict, obsessed with the details of millennial interpretation or apocalyptic symbolism? Not at all. Peter emphasizes the return of Jesus and what will follow because these realities are overwhelmingly precious to him and because they are of the greatest possible practical value to his readers.

'Peter wants to make Christians more heavenly-minded. Nothing will help them more than this' (Edward Donnelly).

Think about it

1. In what practical ways can we encourage each other with the truth of the Second Coming?
2. Look again at Augustine's words above; is this true of you? Do you eagerly await the coming of Christ?

Further reading

W. J. Grier, *The Momentous Event*, Banner of Truth Trust

Quotes

1. Edward Donnelly, *Peter*, Banner of Truth Trust, p.72
2. John Blanchard, *Training for Triumph*, Evangelical Press, p.11
3. Charles Spurgeon, *Sermon*, January 7, 1855
4. C. S. Lewis, *Mere Christianity*, Collins/Fount, p.41
5. A. W. Tozer, *When He is Come*, Send the Light, p.49
6. Stuart Olyott, *The Three are One*, Evangelical Press, p.60
7. John Stott, *Basic Christianity*, IVP, p.62
8. E. F. Kevan, *What the Scriptures Teach*, Evangelical Press, p.31
9. D. M. Lloyd-Jones, *God's Way of Reconciliation*, Evangelical Press, p.130
10. John Murray, *Redemption Accomplished & Applied*, Banner of Truth Trust, p.103
11. Tozer, *Man the Dwelling Place of God*, CPI, p.61
12. J. Packer, *God's Words*, IVP, p.126
13. James M. Boice, *Foundations of the Christian Faith*, IVP, p.329
14. Lloyd-Jones, *Romans 3*, Banner of Truth Trust, p.2
15. J. I. Packer, *Concise theology*, IVP, p.167
16. Stuart Olyott, *The gospel as it really is*, Evangelical Press, p.55
17. Ryle, *Holiness*, James Clarke, pp.19-20
18. Packer, *God's Words, IVP*, p.167
19. D. A. Carson, *John*, IVP, p.393
20. Edward Donnelly, *Peter*, Banner of Truth Trust, p.132

Brief definitions

Atonement. When Jesus died on the cross he bore the punishment of our sin. His blood was shed as a sacrificial offering and so he made amends for our sin.

Propitiation. On the cross Jesus, bearing our sin and guilt, faced the wrath of God instead of us and paid fully on our behalf the debt we owed to the broken law of God. The wrath of God fell upon Jesus, our substitute, instead of upon us.

Grace. This is God showing goodness and mercy to a people who deserve only judgement and condemnation.

Regeneration. In this God gives new life, spiritual life, to those who are dead in sin.

Repentance. The sinner, conscious of his guilt and aware of God's mercy in Christ, turns from his sin to God.

Faith. This is trust in Christ as he is offered to us in the gospel. It is the channel by which salvation comes to us and is, itself, given us by God.

Reconciliation. When two people are in hostility they need to be reconciled. We are reconciled to God when our sin, which causes hostility, is dealt with. Reconciliation replaces hostility with peace.

Redemption. This means to set someone free from captivity or slavery by the payment of a ransom price. We are redeemed from the slavery of sin by the blood of Jesus.

Justification. Only God can justify; we cannot justify ourselves. He does so when he clothes the guilty sinner in the righteousness of Christ and then declares that person to be acceptable to him because of Jesus.

Sanctification. This is a process by which the Christian is purified in heart and mind.

Election. Election simply means that God saves specific individuals.

Eternal security. Not only are we saved by the grace of God but also we cannot lose that salvation. So we are eternally secure.

Knowing your Bible

The only way to know your Bible is to read it every day and to study it.

There is a difference between Bible reading and Bible study; one can be done fairly quickly while the other takes time.

Bible reading

You will need a Bible reading scheme to help you read progressively through Scripture and there are many available. The problem with some of them is that they give you so many chapters to read in a day that you can easily fall behind the schedule. This can so discourage you that you will be tempted to give up. The scheme we recommend in the following pages enables you to read through the New Testament and Psalms in one year by reading just one chapter a day. This is just to start you off and it will be hoped you will want to read more of God's Word as you grow in the faith.

Bible study

Bible study takes time and you will need help to understand the passage you are studying. For a new believer we recommend that you buy the following books and use them as the basis of your study for the first few months after conversion.

John Blanchard, *Read Mark Learn*, Evangelical Press, 45 days study

Peter Jeffery & Owen Milton, *Firm Foundations*, Bryntirion Press, 62 days study

Stuart Olyott, *The gospel as it really is*, Evangelical Press, 26 studies in Romans

John Blanchard, *Luke comes alive*, Evangelical Press, 62 days study

Peter Jeffery, *What you need to know about salvation*, Evangelical Press, 21 days study

Bible reading scheme

A plan to read through the New Testament and the Psalms in a year

Read the set passages prayerfully.
Meditate on the questions each day.
Thank the Lord for his word to you through the passage.

Ask yourself these questions when you read the Scriptures.
1. What does this tell me about God and the Lord Jesus Christ?
2. What lesson can I learn from this passage?
3. What particular sin does it warn me against?
4. What verse, phrase or single word can I take with me for the day?

Day	January	February	March
1	Psalm 1-2	Matthew 17	Galatians 2
2	Psalm 3-4	Matthew 18	Galatians 3
3	Psalm 5	Matthew 19	Galatians 4
4	Psalm 6	Matthew 20	Galatians 5
5	Psalm 7	Matthew 21	Galatians 6
6	Psalm 8	Matthew 22	Revelation 1
7	Psalm 9	Matthew 23	Revelation 2
8	Psalm 10	Matthew 24	Revelation 3
9	Psalm 11-12	Matthew 25	Revelation 4
10	Psalm 13-14	Matthew 26	Revelation 5
11	Psalm 15-16	Matthew 27	Revelation 6
12	Psalm 17	Matthew 28	Revelation 7
13	Psalm 18	Acts 1	Revelation 8
14	Psalm 19	Acts 2	Revelation 9
15	Psalm 20	Acts 3	Revelation 10
16	Psalm 21	Acts 4	Revelation 11
17	Psalm 22	Acts 5	Revelation 12
18	Matthew 1-2	Acts 6	Revelation 13
19	Matthew 3-4	Acts 7	Revelation 14
20	Matthew 5	Acts 8	Revelation 15
21	Matthew 6	Acts 9	Revelation 16
22	Matthew 7	Acts 10	Revelation 17
23	Matthew 8	Acts 11	Revelation 18
24	Matthew 9	Acts 12	Revelation 19
25	Matthew 10	Acts 13	Revelation 20
26	Matthew 11	Acts 14	Revelation 21
27	Matthew 12	Acts 15	Revelation 22
28	Matthew 13	Galatians 1	Mark 1
29	Matthew 14		Mark 2
30	Matthew 15		Mark 3
31	Matthew 16		Mark 4

Bible reading plan

Day	April	May	June
1	Mark 5	2 Timothy 1	Romans 15
2	Mark 6	2 Timothy 2	Romans 16
3	Mark 7	2 Timothy 3-4	James 1
4	Mark 8	Titus 1	James 2
5	Mark 9	Acts 16	James 3
6	Mark 10	Acts 17	James 4
7	Mark 11	Acts 18	James 5
8	Mark 12	Acts 19	Psalm 36
9	Mark 13	Acts 20	Psalm 37
10	Mark 14	Acts 21	Psalm 38
11	Mark 15	Acts 22	Psalm 39
12	Mark 16	Acts 23	Psalm 40
13	Psalm 23-24	Acts 24	Psalm 41
14	Psalm 25	Acts 25	Psalm 42
15	Psalm 26	Acts 26	Psalm 43
16	Psalm 27	Acts 27	Psalm 44
17	Psalm 28	Acts 28	1 Corinthians 1
18	Psalm 29	Romans 1	1 Corinthians 2
19	Psalm 30	Romans 2	1 Corinthians 3
20	Psalm 31	Romans 3	1 Corinthians 4
21	Psalm 32	Romans 4	1 Corinthians 5
22	Psalm 33	Romans 5	1 Corinthians 6
23	Psalm 34	Romans 6	1 Corinthians 7
24	Psalm 35	Romans 7	1 Corinthians 8
25	1 Timothy 1	Romans 8	1 Corinthians 9
26	1 Timothy 2	Romans 9	1 Corinthians 10
27	1 Timothy 3	Romans 10	1 Corinthians 11
28	1 Timothy 4	Romans 11	1 Corinthians 12
29	1 Timothy 5	Romans 12	1 Corinthians 13
30	1 Timothy 6	Romans 13	1 Corinthians 14
31		Romans 14	

Day	July	August	September
1	1 Corinthians 15	Luke 23	Hebrews 1
2	1 Corinthians 16	Luke 24	Hebrews 2
3	2 Corinthians 1-2	Philippians 1	Hebrews 3
4	2 Corinthians 3-4	Philippians 2	Hebrews 4
5	2 Corinthians 5-6	Philippians 3	Hebrews 5
6	2 Corinthians 7-8	Philippians 4	Hebrews 6
7	2 Corinthians 9-10	1 Thessalonians 1	Hebrews 7
8	2 Corinthians 11	1 Thessalonians 2-3	Hebrews 8
9	2 Corinthians 12-13	1 Thessalonians 4-5	Hebrews 9
10	Luke 1	2 Thessalonians 1-3	Hebrews 10
11	Luke 2	Psalm 45	Hebrews 11
12	Luke 3	Psalm 46-47	Hebrews 12
13	Luke 4	Psalm 48	Hebrews 13
14	Luke 5	Psalm 49	Ephesians 1
15	Luke 6	Psalm 50	Ephesians 2
16	Luke 7	Psalm 51	Ephesians 3
17	Luke 8	Psalm 52	Ephesians 4
18	Luke 9	Psalm 53	Ephesians 5
19	Luke 10	Psalm 54	Ephesians 6
20	Luke 11	Psalm 55	Colossians 1
21	Luke 12	Psalm 56	Colossians 2
22	Luke 13	Psalm 57	Colossians 3
23	Luke 14	Psalm 58	Colossians 4
24	Luke 15	Psalm 59	John 1
25	Luke 16	Psalm 60-61	John 2
26	Luke 17	Psalm 62-63	John 3
27	Luke 18	Psalm 64-65	John 4
28	Luke 19	Psalm 66-67	John 5
29	Luke 20	Psalm 68	John 6
30	Luke 21	Psalm 69	John 7
31	Luke 22	Psalm 70-71	

Day	October	November	December
1	John 8	Psalm 73	Psalm 119 73-104
2	John 9	Psalm 74	Psalm 119 105-136
3	John 10	Psalm 75	Psalm 119 137-176
4	John 11	Psalm 76	Psalm 120-122
5	John 12	Psalm 77	Psalm 123-125
6	John 13	Psalm 78	Psalm 126-128
7	John 14	Psalm 79-80	Psalm 129-132
8	John 15	Psalm 81-82	Psalm 133-135
9	John 16	Psalm 83-84	Psalm 136-137
10	John 17	Psalm 85-86	Psalm 138-139
11	John 18	Psalm 87-88	Psalm 140
12	John 19	Psalm 89	Psalm 141
13	John 20	Psalm 90-91	Psalm 142
14	John 21	Psalm 92-93	Psalm 143
15	Philemon	Psalm 94-95	Psalm 144
16	1 Peter 1	Psalm 96-97	Psalm 145
17	1 Peter 2	Psalm 98-99	Psalm 146
18	1 Peter 3	Psalm 100-101	Psalm 147
19	1 Peter 4	Psalm 102	Psalm 148
20	1 Peter 5	Psalm 103	Psalm 149
21	2 Peter 1	Psalm 104	Psalm 150
22	2 Peter 2	Psalm 105	Matthew 1
23	2 Peter 3	Psalm 106	Matthew 2:1-12
24	1 John 1	Psalm 107-108	Matthew 2:13-22
25	1 John 2	Psalm 109-110	John 1:1-14
26	1 John 3	Psalm 111-113	Luke 1:1-24
27	1 John 4	Psalm 114-116	Luke 1:25-56
28	1 John 5	Psalm 117-118	Luke 1:57-80
29	2 John	Psalm 119 1-32	Luke 2:1-20
30	3 John	Psalm 119 33-72	Luke 2:21-40
31	Psalm 72		Luke 2:41-52

A wide range of excellent books on spiritual subjects is available from Evangelical Press. Please write to us for your free catalogue or contact us by e-mail.

Evangelical Press
Faverdale North Industrial Estate, Darlington, Co. Durham, DL3 0PH, England

Evangelical Press USA
P. O. Box 84, Auburn, MA 01501, USA

e-mail: sales@evangelical-press.org

web: www.evangelical-press.org